THE BEST OF
DILBERT™
VOLUME 1

Selected cartoons from SHAVE THE WHALES
by Scott Adams

SCOTT ADAMS

BXTREE

First published 2002 by Boxtree
an imprint of Pan Macmillan Ltd
Pan Macmillan, 20 New Wharf Road, London N1 9RR
Basingstoke and Oxford
Associated companies throughout the world
www.panmacmillan.com

ISBN 0 7522 6541 5

1 3 5 7 9 8 6 4 2

A CIP catalogue record for this book is available from the British Library.

Printed and bound in Great Britain by
Mackays of Chatham plc, Chatham, Kent

For Pam, my role model

INTRODUCTION

You may think this book is simply a cynical way to cash in on the popularity of the strip without doing much of anything in the way of extra work. And you'd be largely correct about that. But look at it this way: After you enjoy it, you can give it to somebody else as a gift. That's something you can't do with, say, a bottle of wine (at least not gracefully). A Dilbert book is a rare opportunity to satisfy your greed and your nagging gift-giving guilt at the same time. It's a win-win scenario.

The only problem is that the book doesn't quite lay flat after you've pawed your way through it. You'll need an alibi.

I recommend that you get a felt-tipped pen and write "Best Wishes — Scott Adams" on the inside cover and try to pass it off as an autographed copy. You could even sketch a little Dogbert in there. If he looks a little deformed, just say my arm was in a sling.*

If the recipient hunts me down to verify your clam, I'll lie for you. You have my word on that.

On a related topic, many of you have written to ask how you can join a Dilbert/Dogbert fan club, mailing list, cult, or paramilitary force. So far, all we have is a mailing list. There are two benefits to being on the mailing list:
1.) You get a free Dilbert newsletter if we feel like it, and
2.) When Dogbert conquers the world, you will form a new ruling class.

To get on the mailing list, write:

E-mail: scottadams@aol.com

Snail Mail: Dilbert Mailing List
            United Media
            200 Park Avenue
            New York, NY 10166

Scott Adams

*If it looks better than I draw it, I hate you.

ALL MAMMALS HAVE HAIR.
WHALES ARE MAMMALS...
THEREFORE, WHALES HAVE HAIR.
SHAVE THE WHALES.

UH OH... DOUBLE DOORS. ONE SIDE IS ALWAYS LOCKED AND I MAKE A FOOL OF MYSELF TRYING TO OPEN IT.
WHICH SIDE IS IT? LEFT? RIGHT? PEOPLE ARE WATCHING. THINK, THINK...
S.Adams
THAT'S WHEN I NOTICED THAT THE VENTILATION DUCTS WERE BIG ENOUGH FOR A HUMAN TO CRAWL THROUGH.
TOO BAD THEY DIDN'T LEAD OUTSIDE.

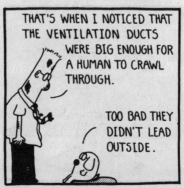

HERE'S AN INTERESTING EDITORIAL . . .
NEWS
THIS GUY SAYS WE SHOULD INCREASE THE PAY OF CONGRESSMEN TO REMOVE INCENTIVE FOR THEM TO ENGAGE IN ILLEGAL ACTS.
NEWS
BY THAT THEORY, CRIMINALS AREN'T BAD, JUST UNDER-PAID.
NEWS
S. Adams

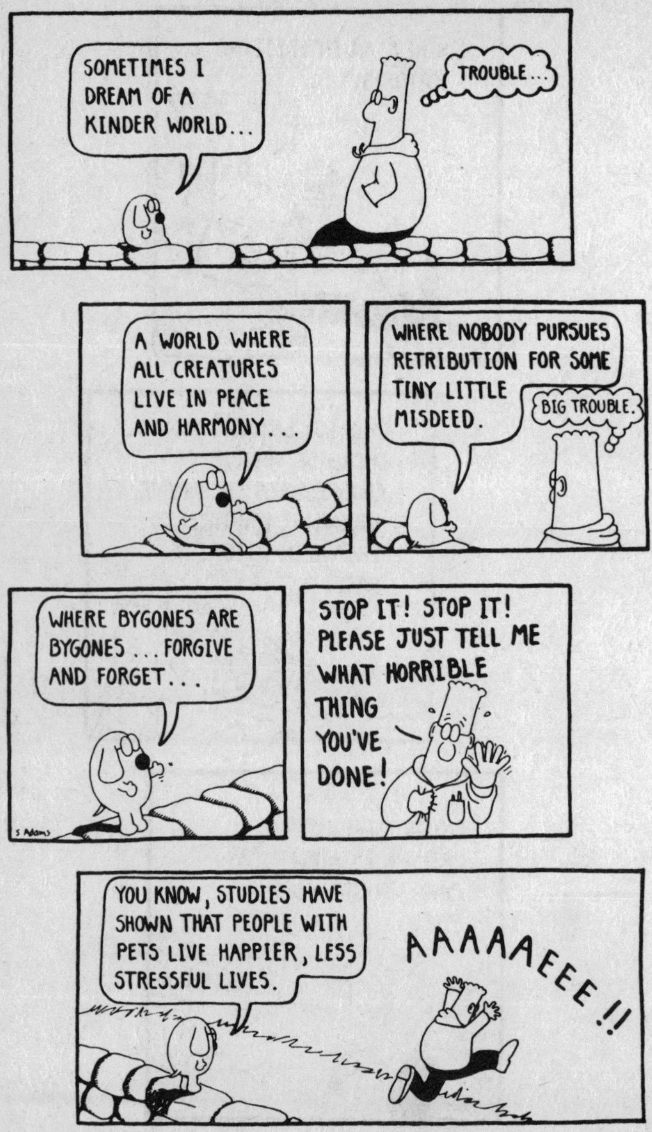
SOMETIMES I DREAM OF A KINDER WORLD...
TROUBLE...
A WORLD WHERE ALL CREATURES LIVE IN PEACE AND HARMONY...
WHERE NOBODY PURSUES RETRIBUTION FOR SOME TINY LITTLE MISDEED.
BIG TROUBLE.
WHERE BYGONES ARE BYGONES ... FORGIVE AND FORGET...
S Adams
STOP IT! STOP IT! PLEASE JUST TELL ME WHAT HORRIBLE THING YOU'VE DONE!
YOU KNOW, STUDIES HAVE SHOWN THAT PEOPLE WITH PETS LIVE HAPPIER, LESS STRESSFUL LIVES.
AAAAAEEEE!!

HOLD IT RIGHT THERE, FELLA!
UH-OH... YOU MUST HAVE SEEN ME EAT THAT GRAPE IN AISLE "B."
I JUST WANT TO MAKE SURE YOU PAY FOR IT.
LOOKS LIKE 192 POUNDS. WHAT WERE YOU BEFORE YOU CAME IN?
HAPPY.

SCIENTISTS HAVE DISCOVERED THE GENE THAT MAKES SOME PEOPLE LOVE GOLF.
HOW CAN THEY TELL IT'S THE GOLF GENE ?
IT'S PLAID AND IT LIES.
I PROBABLY SHOULDN'T RELY ON YOU FOR MY SCIENCE UPDATES.

MY TERRARIUM EXPERIMENT IS A FAILURE.
BY NOW IT SHOULD HAVE STARTED ITS OWN SELF-CONTAINED WEATHER PATTERNS.
S.Adams
AFTER ALL THIS WAITING, IT'S JUST SO... SO...
ANTI-CLIMATIC?

ISN'T IT STUPID THAT THE WORLD ECONOMY IS BASED ON GOLD?
YEAH... NO MATTER HOW ADVANCED CIVILIZATION GETS, WE STILL USE ROCKS FOR MONEY.
THE DUMB PART IS USING A ROCK THAT'S SO HARD TO FIND.

I WISH THIS GUY WOULDN'T TRY TO BE POLITE AND HOLD THE DOOR.
I'M AT THAT AWKWARD DISTANCE WHERE I SHOULD LUNGE FORWARD SO HE DOESN'T HAVE TO HOLD THE DOOR TOO LONG.
OH, THANK YOU.
S.ADAMS
GREAT. NOW I'M LATE.
I LUNGED AS FAST AS I COULD. SORRY.

HEY, HOW ARE YOU? WHAT'S HAPPENIN'?
GOOD TO SEE YOU. I'M FINE. GREAT, GREAT. TAKE CARE.
I GUESS THERE WAS NO REAL NEED FOR ME TO PARTICIPATE IN THAT.
S.Adams

OKAY THEN, SUPPOSE YOU HAD EVERYTHING YOU WANTED. WHAT WOULD YOU DO?
GLOAT. MAKE EVERY-BODY ELSE FEEL LIKE FAILURES. LIVE A GARISH AND DECADENT LIFE.
S. Adams
AND WHEN THAT GETS BORING?
MAYBE START MY OWN PERFUME COMPANY.

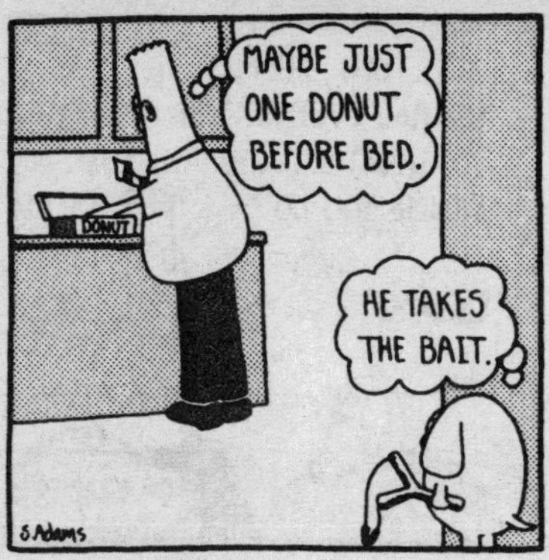
MAYBE JUST ONE DONUT BEFORE BED.
DONUT
HE TAKES THE BAIT.
S. Adams

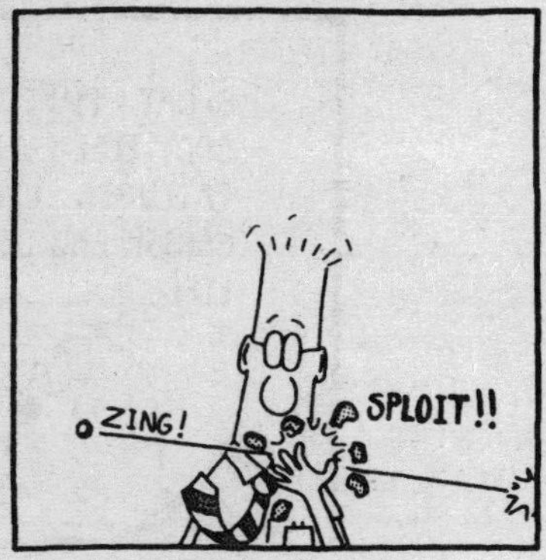
ZING!
SPLOIT!!

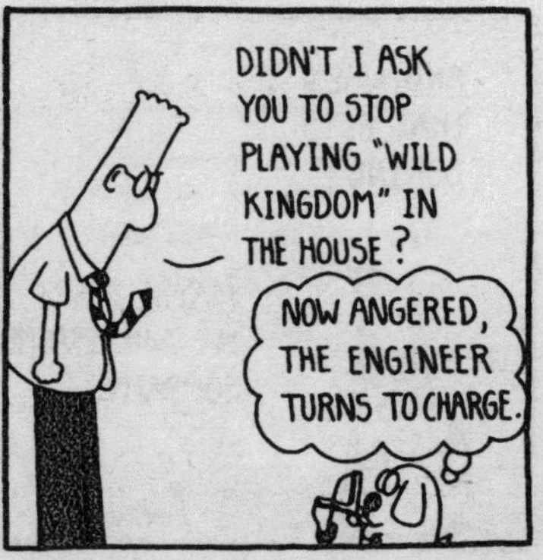
DIDN'T I ASK YOU TO STOP PLAYING "WILD KINGDOM" IN THE HOUSE?
NOW ANGERED, THE ENGINEER TURNS TO CHARGE.

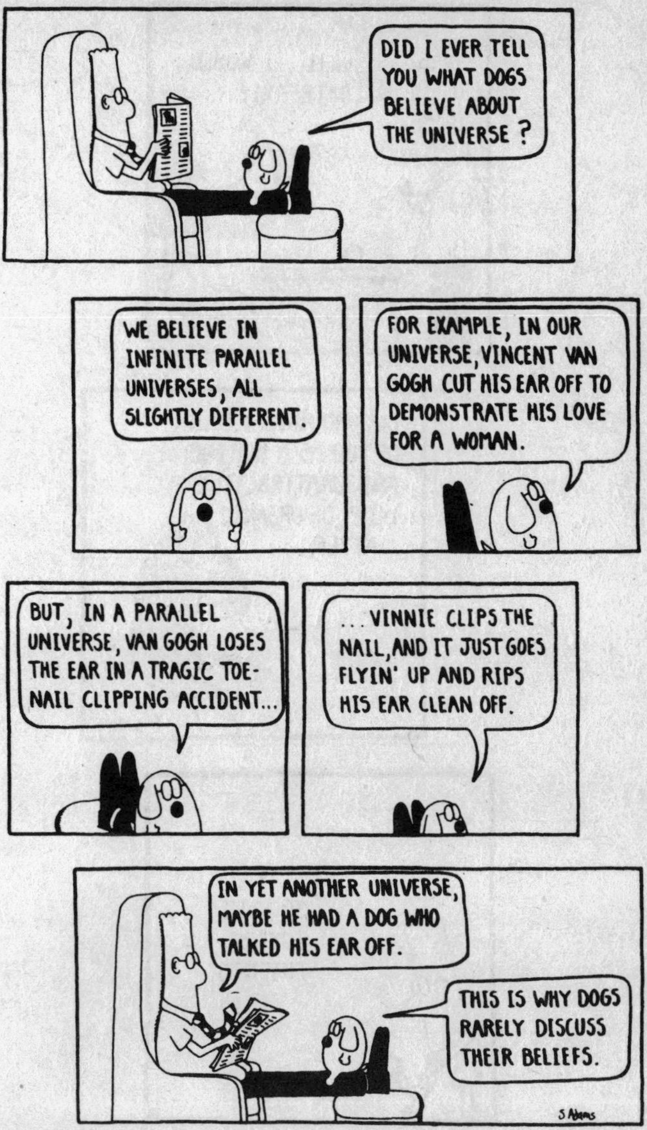
DID I EVER TELL YOU WHAT DOGS BELIEVE ABOUT THE UNIVERSE ?
WE BELIEVE IN INFINITE PARALLEL UNIVERSES, ALL SLIGHTLY DIFFERENT.
FOR EXAMPLE, IN OUR UNIVERSE, VINCENT VAN GOGH CUT HIS EAR OFF TO DEMONSTRATE HIS LOVE FOR A WOMAN.
BUT, IN A PARALLEL UNIVERSE, VAN GOGH LOSES THE EAR IN A TRAGIC TOE-NAIL CLIPPING ACCIDENT...
...VINNIE CLIPS THE NAIL, AND IT JUST GOES FLYIN' UP AND RIPS HIS EAR CLEAN OFF.
IN YET ANOTHER UNIVERSE, MAYBE HE HAD A DOG WHO TALKED HIS EAR OFF.
THIS IS WHY DOGS RARELY DISCUSS THEIR BELIEFS.
S Adams

WELL... I WOULD DATE YOU...
BUT FRANKLY I THINK OF YOU AS A BORING AND UNATTRACTIVE BLOB OF ORGANIC MATTER...
S.Adams
SO LET'S JUST BE FRIENDS.

PARDON ME, SIR, BUT I COULDN'T HELP NOTICING THESE EQUATIONS IN YOUR GARBAGE.
I TOOK THE LIBERTY OF CORRECTING A FEW QUANTUM CALCULATIONS.
S. Adams
GOSH. WHY ARE YOU A GARBAGE MAN?
I THINK THE QUESTION IS "WHY ARE YOU AN ENGINEER?"

I UNDERSTAND YOU'RE THE WORLD'S SMARTEST GARBAGE MAN.
I'M DOGBERT, THE WORLD'S SMARTEST DOG; ACCORDING TO ME, ANYWAY.
I JUST WONDERED WHY YOU CHOOSE TO BE A GARBAGE MAN.
I THINK IT WAS THE GLAMOUR WHICH FIRST INTRIGUED ME.

GOD SPOKE TO ME TODAY. HE APPOINTED ME RULER OF ALL CREATURES ON EARTH.
GOD DID NOT SPEAK TO YOU.
IT WAS WORTH A SHOT.
S.Adams

DOGBERT PLAYS A RECKLESS PRANK WITH DILBERT'S PROTO-TYPE "HOT LINE" TO THE KREMLIN.

HEY GORBY, DID YOU HEAR THIS QUOTE...

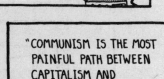

"COMMUNISM IS THE MOST PAINFUL PATH BETWEEN CAPITALISM AND CAPITALISM."

"FIRE ONE"? HA HA HA...WHAT A KIDDER YOU ARE.

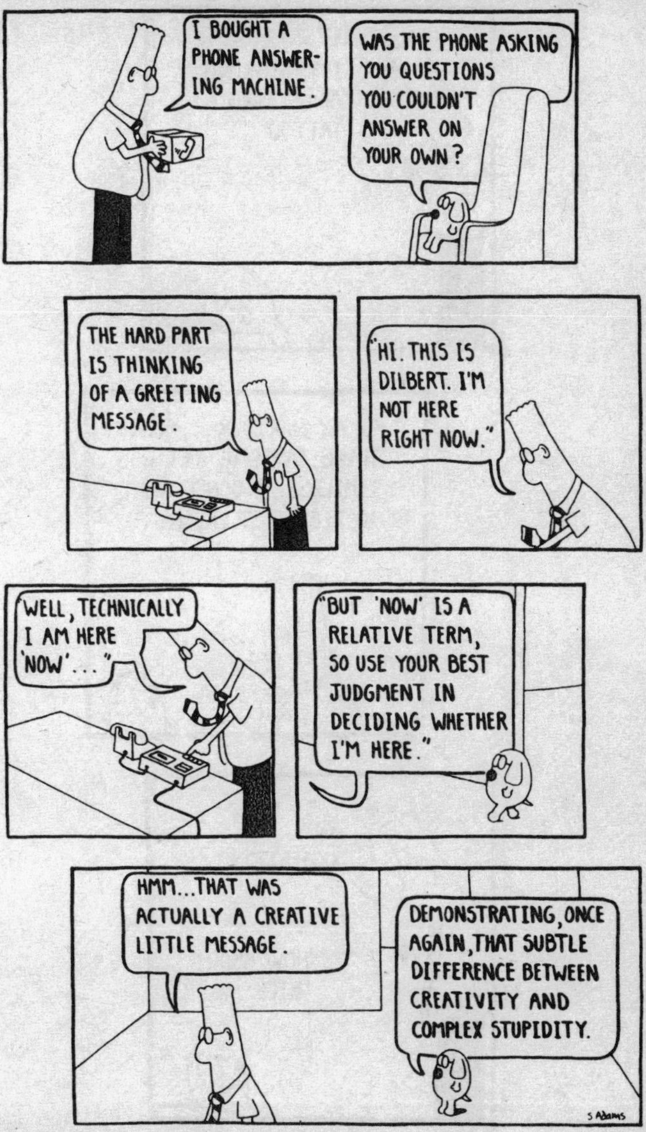
I BOUGHT A PHONE ANSWERING MACHINE.
WAS THE PHONE ASKING YOU QUESTIONS YOU COULDN'T ANSWER ON YOUR OWN?
THE HARD PART IS THINKING OF A GREETING MESSAGE.
"HI. THIS IS DILBERT. I'M NOT HERE RIGHT NOW."
"WELL, TECHNICALLY I AM HERE 'NOW'..."
"BUT 'NOW' IS A RELATIVE TERM, SO USE YOUR BEST JUDGMENT IN DECIDING WHETHER I'M HERE."
HMM...THAT WAS ACTUALLY A CREATIVE LITTLE MESSAGE.
DEMONSTRATING, ONCE AGAIN, THAT SUBTLE DIFFERENCE BETWEEN CREATIVITY AND COMPLEX STUPIDITY.
S Adams

I'M THINKING OF GETTING A TATTOO.
ON MY SHOULDER... SOMETHING TASTEFUL YET TIMELESS. I DON'T WANT TO REGRET IT LATER.
S.Adams
ANY SUGGESTIONS?
HOW ABOUT "KICK ME"?

I'M GRUMPY TODAY, SO DON'T EVEN TRY TO TALK TO ME.
NEWS
S.Adams
AND DON'T TRY TO FLATTER ME OR GIVE ME CHOCOLATE CAKE TO MAKE ME FEEL BETTER.
AND I GUESS I SHOULDN'T SCRATCH YOU BEHIND THE EARS UNTIL YOU HAVE LITTLE LEG SPASMS.
RIGHT. NONE OF THAT.

I'M STARTING TO WRITE AN UNAUTHORIZED BIOGRAPHY ABOUT YOU.
IT'S KIND OF A "PET AND TELL" EXPOSÉ FULL OF STARTLING REVELATIONS.
S. Adams
WHO WOULD BE STARTLED BY MY LIFE?
I THINK YOU WILL BE.

ARE YOU REALLY GOING THROUGH WITH THE UNAUTHORIZED BIOGRAPHY OF ME?
YES.
S.Adams
I'M UP TO THE PART WHERE JACKIE "O" AND LIZ TAYLOR FIGHT A DUEL FOR YOUR LOVE.
TRAGICALLY, NEITHER ARE AWARE THAT YOU'RE CARRYING STEVE GARVEY'S BABY!
TAP
TAP
TAP

I CAN FEEL THE STATIC ELECTRICITY BUILDING . . .
SHUFFLE SHUFFLE
SHUFFLE SHUFFLE
SHUFFLE
SHUFFLE
SHUFFLE
SHUFFLE
I MOST CERTAINLY WILL NOT CALL YOU "THOR, DOG OF THUNDER."
PREPARE TO DIE.
S. Adams

MAYBE SINCE YOU'RE FULL OF STATIC ELECTRICITY, YOU SHOULD SAY "IT IS USELESS TO BE A RESISTOR." HEE-HEE-HEE.
S. Adams
ZAP!!
NOTHING ANNOYS THE "DOG OF THUNDER" QUITE AS MUCH AS NERD PUNS.

LET'S GO...IT'S TIME TO RENEW YOUR DOG LICENSE.
DEPARTMENT OF DOGS
I WONDER WHAT HAPPENS IF I FAIL THE WRITTEN TEST?
S. Adams

I'M SORRY, BUT IT SEEMS YOU'VE FAILED THE WRITTEN PORTION OF THE DOG LICENSE TEST.
IMPOSSIBLE!
FOR EXAMPLE, THIS QUESTION ON "NATURAL ENEMIES": THE CORRECT ANSWER IS "MAILMAN." YOU WROTE-IN "FAX MACHINE."
S.Adams
HOW'D IT GO?
THE "DEPARTMENT OF DOGS" DOES NOT KEEP UP WITH EMERGING TRENDS.

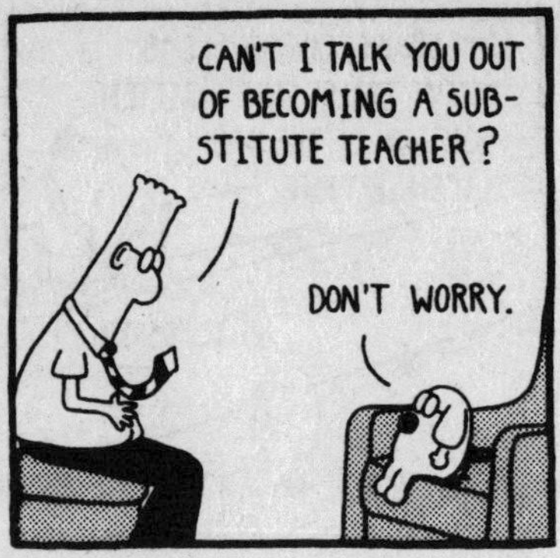
CAN'T I TALK YOU OUT OF BECOMING A SUB-STITUTE TEACHER?
DON'T WORRY.

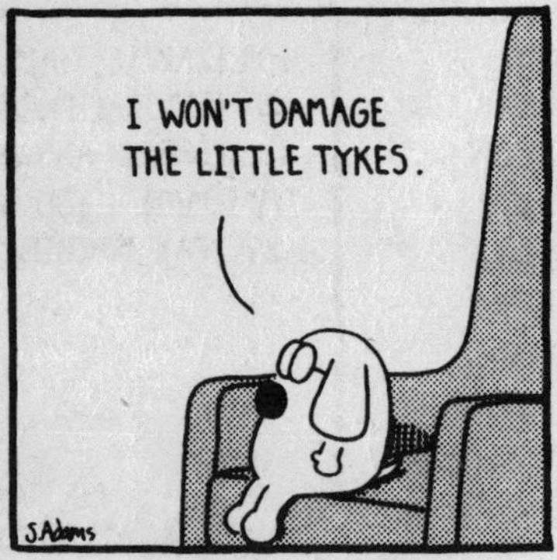
I WON'T DAMAGE THE LITTLE TYKES.
S.Adams

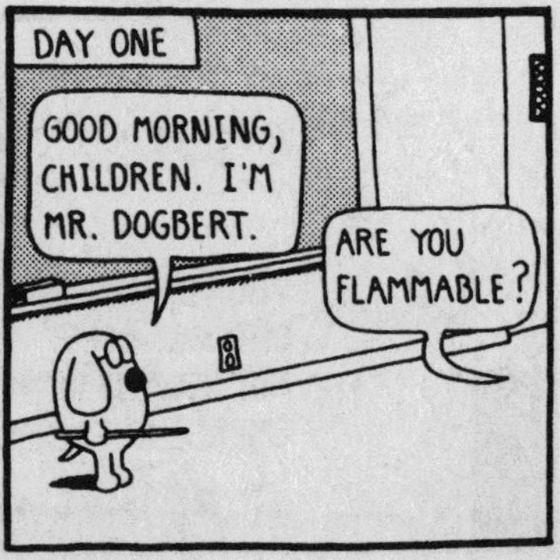
DAY ONE
GOOD MORNING, CHILDREN. I'M MR. DOGBERT.
ARE YOU FLAMMABLE?

DAY ONE AS A SUBSTITUTE TEACHER
JENNIFER! PUT THAT FLAME-THROWER AWAY RIGHT THIS MINUTE!
EUGENE! RELEASE THOSE HOSTAGES OR I SHALL BE FORCED TO FLING THIS CHALK ERASER AT YOUR HEAD!
S. Adams
IS THAT A "STINGER" MISSILE LAUNCHER? WELL, I HOPE YOU BROUGHT ENOUGH FOR EVERYBODY!
I DID.

OKAY, CLASS . . . PUT YOUR WEAPONS AWAY AND OPEN YOUR TV GUIDES.
TIMMY, PLEASE READ ALOUD THE PASSAGE FROM "FALCON CREST" UNDER THE FRIDAY LISTINGS.
THERE'S GOT TO BE A BETTER WAY TO TEACH SEX EDUCATION.
S.Adams

HOW WAS YOUR FIRST DAY AS A SUBSTITUTE SCHOOL TEACHER?
IMAGINE FEELING COMPLETELY POWER-LESS . . . LIKE A MARBLE STATUE . . .
S.Adams
GOSH... THAT SOUNDS PRETTY BAD.
NOW IMAGINE THE BIGGEST FLOCK OF PIGEONS YOU EVER SAW...

I THINK I'M LOSING MY HAIR.
DON'T BE SILLY. YOU AREN'T LOSING YOUR HAIR.
I'M NOT? OH, GOOD.
HOW COULD YOU POSSIBLY LOSE THESE HUGE CLUMPS...

NORMALLY I'D GIVE YOU SIX MONTHS TO LIVE.
BUT WE'RE HAVING A "50% OFF SALE" TODAY, SO I'LL GIVE YOU A FULL YEAR FOR THE SAME PRICE.
AND YOU GET AN EXTRA TEN DAYS IF YOU PAY CASH!
S.Adams

...AND THE DOCTOR GAVE ME JUST A YEAR TO LIVE.
I'M SORRY, LITTLE GUY... I DON'T KNOW HOW YOU'LL MANAGE WITH-OUT ME.
WOULD IT BE TOO MUCH TROUBLE TO PAINT THE HOUSE BEFORE YOU GO?
S. Adams

IT SEEMS WE HAD A MIX-UP WITH YOUR TEST RESULTS.
THEN I'M NOT DYING?
S.ADAMS
WE DOCTORS ARE AMAZINGLY SMART, BUT OCCASIONALLY WE MAKE A LITTLE ERROR.
WELL... I UNDERSTAND.
BY THE WAY, YOUR PAP SMEAR WAS NORMAL.

BY MY CALCULATIONS, WE CAN MAKE MILLIONS BY COMBINING A MORTUARY BUSINESS AND A GARBAGE COLLECTION BUSINESS.
S.Adams
OUR CUSTOMERS COULD SIMPLY LEAVE THE DEARLY DEPARTED BY THE CURB FOR PICK-UP.
MAYBE WE COULD ADD PIZZA DELIVERY, TOO.
LET'S NOT PUSH A GOOD IDEA TOO FAR.

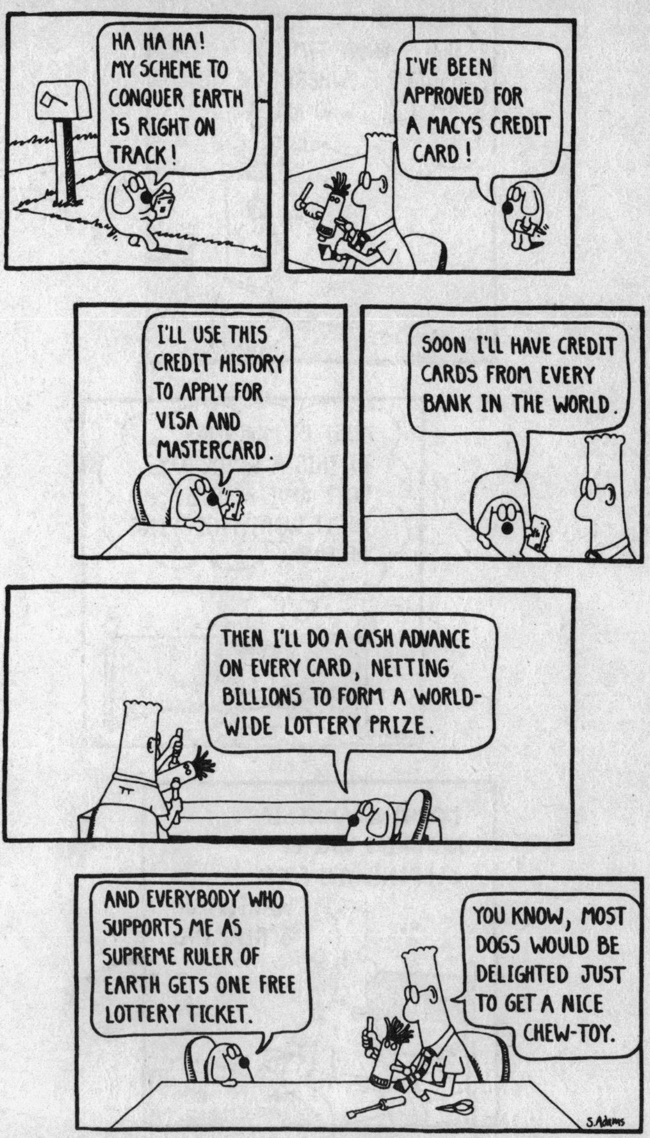
HA HA HA!
MY SCHEME TO CONQUER EARTH IS RIGHT ON TRACK!
I'VE BEEN APPROVED FOR A MACYS CREDIT CARD!
I'LL USE THIS CREDIT HISTORY TO APPLY FOR VISA AND MASTERCARD.
SOON I'LL HAVE CREDIT CARDS FROM EVERY BANK IN THE WORLD.
THEN I'LL DO A CASH ADVANCE ON EVERY CARD, NETTING BILLIONS TO FORM A WORLD-WIDE LOTTERY PRIZE.
AND EVERYBODY WHO SUPPORTS ME AS SUPREME RULER OF EARTH GETS ONE FREE LOTTERY TICKET.
YOU KNOW, MOST DOGS WOULD BE DELIGHTED JUST TO GET A NICE CHEW-TOY.
S. Adams

UGH... WHAT TIME IS IT? ...WHERE AM I?...WHO AM I?
MUST BE MORNING... IS THIS A WORK DAY? DO I HAVE A JOB?... IS IT WORTH GETTING UP FOR?
S.Adams
"MORNING AMNESIA": NATURE'S WAY OF KEEPING YOU FROM
WAKING UP SCREAMING.

DOGBERT, WE CAN'T STAND HIDING AROUND THE HOUSE ANYMORE.
WE DINOSAURS RULED THIS PLANET ONCE. NOW WE JUST HIDE IN PEOPLE'S HOUSES, PRETENDING TO BE EXTINCT.
S.Adams
DAWN, IT'S TIME FOR OUR COMEBACK TOUR.
I THINK SOME OF ELVIS' JUMPSUITS WILL FIT.

WE'LL KICK OFF THE DINOSAUR COMEBACK TOUR BY SINGING "MY WAY."
THEN WE'LL BREAK THE INSTRUMENTS, WADE INTO THE CROWD AND BITE THE HEAD OFF SOMEBODY IN THE FRONT ROW!
S. Adams
"OZZY OSBOURNE" ALREADY DID THAT.

ICE CREAM
S.Adams
LOOK OUT!
SORRY. I'VE BEEN REALLY JUMPY EVER SINCE THE ICE AGE CAUGHT ME OFF GUARD.

YOU'VE HEARD THE "OTHER" TIRE COMPANY IMPLY THAT YOUR CHILD'S SAFETY DEPENDS ON ITS PRODUCT...
THAT'S NOTHING. IF YOU DON'T BUY OUR TIRES YOUR WHOLE STINKIN' EXTENDED FAMILY WILL CROAK!!!
S.Adams
AND DON'T GET TOO ATTACHED TO THE FAMILY DOG, EITHER. HA HA HA HA HA!!

DOGBERT...
NAPPING
AGAIN?
DON'T YOU KNOW THAT MANY FAMOUS PEOPLE FUNCTIONED WITH VERY LITTLE SLEEP...?
THERE WERE JACKIE GLEASON, BEN FRANKLIN, NAPOLEON...
I LIKE TO THINK I'M MORE ATTRACTIVE THAN ANY OF THOSE GUYS.

...SO TO DO OUR PART FOR EAST-WEST RELATIONS...
S.Adams
I'VE DECIDED TO HOST A DOG FROM THE SOVIET EX-CHANGE PROGRAM.
WHAT?
DOGBERT, I'D LIKE YOU TO MEET NIKITA... NIKITA DORGACHEV.
CHARMED.

DOGBERT MEETS THE SOVIET-EXCHANGE PROGRAM DOG.
HE SEEMS HARMLESS.
GREETINGS, COMRADE DOGBERT.
I HAVE COME TO LEARN CAPITALIST SYSTEM FROM DOG'S PERSPECTIVE.
S.Adams
...AND YOUR GOD IS THIS DONALD TRUMP?
I DON'T THINK IT'S OFFICIAL YET.

YOU SEE, DORGY, UNDER OUR CAPITALIST SYSTEM ANYBODY CAN BECOME RICH.
HOW?
S.Adams
INHERITANCE AND CRIME ARE THE MOST POPULAR METHODS.
WHICH IS PREFERRED METHOD?
IT'S BEST TO HAVE YOUR PARENTS DO THE CRIME AND LET YOU INHERIT IT.

DORGY, WHY ARE YOU DRESSED LIKE A MAID?
DOGBERT IS TEACHING ME CAPITALISM.
TODAY I AM LOWLY MAID. BUT WITH HARD WORK I WILL BE PROMOTED TO JOB AS MAJOR INDUST-RIALIST.
RIGHT?
S.Adams
APPARENTLY THERE IS FLAW IN SYSTEM.
YEAH, BUT WE BLAME IT ON THE JAPANESE.

HELLO, IS THIS THE LIBRARY REFERENCE DESK?
YES.
S.Adams
WHAT'S THE AVERAGE RUNNING SPEED OF THE TAZMANIAN BOOLA-BOOLA DOG?
8.3 MILES PER HOUR.
I CAN'T BELIEVE SHE KNEW THAT.
AND YOU HAVE SOME-THING STUCK IN YOUR TEETH.

DOESN'T "FAST" MEAN NOT EATING?
SO HOW CAN YOU HAVE "FAST FOOD"?
AND HOW MUCH WOULD I HAVE TO EAT BEFORE I STARVED TO DEATH?

MISTER GARBAGE MAN, WHAT IS LIFE ?
WELL, DOGBERT...
LIFE IS LIKE OLD CANTALOUPE RINDS WRAPPED IN A FADED NEWSPAPER AND SPRINKLED WITH WET COFFEE GROUNDS.
S.Adams
LIFE IS GARBAGE ?
CALL ME A ROMANTIC.

I CAN TELL WHAT MY DATE IS THINKING BY HER BODY LANGUAGE.
S. Adams
HER BODY IS TELLING ME "LET'S CUDDLE BY A FIREPLACE..."
"I'LL GET SOME FIREWOOD," SHE SAYS...
VROOOOOM

YO! DILBERT AND DOGBERT!
OH NO...
HI, VERNON.
YO.
THE MOST BORING PERSON I KNOW... GOTTA GET OUT OF HERE BUT I'M TOO POLITE.
DID I EVER TELL YOU ABOUT MY FAVORITE EPISODE OF "KOJAK"?
THERE'S ALWAYS THE DIRECT METHOD.
WHOA! VERN, WE GOTTA GO BEFORE YOU TURN OUR BRAINS INTO TAPIOCA!

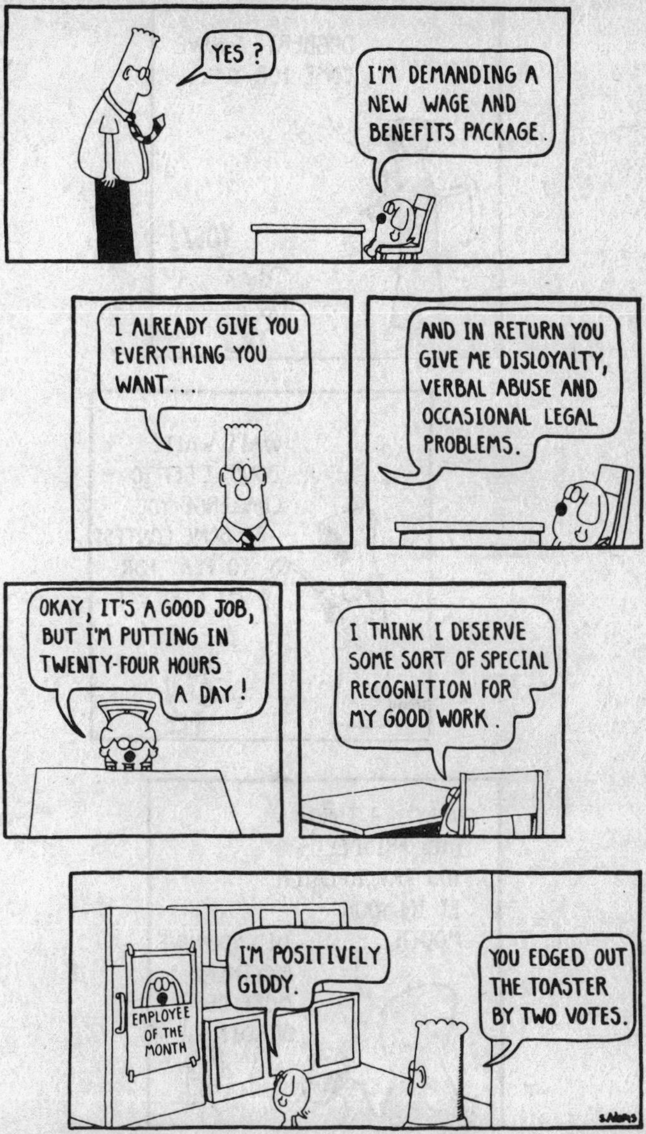
YES ?
I'M DEMANDING A NEW WAGE AND BENEFITS PACKAGE.
I ALREADY GIVE YOU EVERYTHING YOU WANT. . .
AND IN RETURN YOU GIVE ME DISLOYALTY, VERBAL ABUSE AND OCCASIONAL LEGAL PROBLEMS.
OKAY, IT'S A GOOD JOB, BUT I'M PUTTING IN TWENTY-FOUR HOURS A DAY !
I THINK I DESERVE SOME SORT OF SPECIAL RECOGNITION FOR MY GOOD WORK.
EMPLOYEE OF THE MONTH
I'M POSITIVELY GIDDY.
YOU EDGED OUT THE TOASTER BY TWO VOTES.

DOGBERT, I HAVE COME FOR YOU.
YOW!
WAIT WAIT! DON'T I GET TO CHALLENGE YOU TO SOME CONTEST TO PLAY FOR MY LIFE !!?
S.ADAMS
OKAY... I THROW THIS FRISBEE - YOU TRY TO CATCH IT IN YOUR MOUTH.
DID YOU HAVE ANYTHING MORE DE-GRADING ?

DOGBERT TRIES TO CHEAT DEATH.
...SO, IF YOU CATCH THE FRISBEE YOU CAN LIVE.
WAIT!
I'VE NEVER BEEN MUCH OF AN ATHLETE... LET'S PLAY "SCRABBLE" FOR MY LIFE INSTEAD.
S.Adams
HOW MUCH TIME ARE YOU ALLOWED FOR YOUR TURN?
I'LL SEE YOU IN AUGUST, BONE BOY.

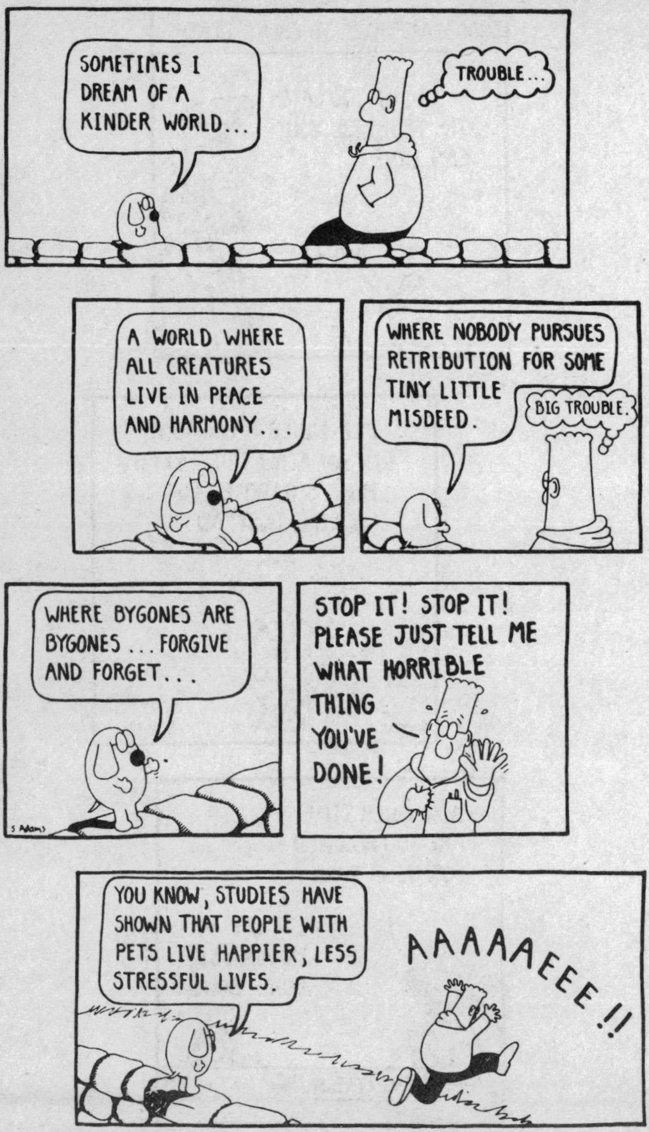
SOMETIMES I DREAM OF A KINDER WORLD...
TROUBLE...
A WORLD WHERE ALL CREATURES LIVE IN PEACE AND HARMONY...
WHERE NOBODY PURSUES RETRIBUTION FOR SOME TINY LITTLE MISDEED.
BIG TROUBLE.
WHERE BYGONES ARE BYGONES ... FORGIVE AND FORGET...
S Adams
STOP IT! STOP IT! PLEASE JUST TELL ME WHAT HORRIBLE THING YOU'VE DONE!
YOU KNOW, STUDIES HAVE SHOWN THAT PEOPLE WITH PETS LIVE HAPPIER, LESS STRESSFUL LIVES.
AAAAAEEEE!!

REMEMBER, ONE OF YOUR DUTIES AS DOG IS TO GUARD THE HOUSE.
S.Adams
THAT MIGHT ENTAIL RIPPING INTRUDERS TO BITS WITH YOUR TEETH... OR TAKING A BULLET FOR ME.
BOY, ALL THAT AND I GET TO DRINK OUT OF THE TOILET TOO.

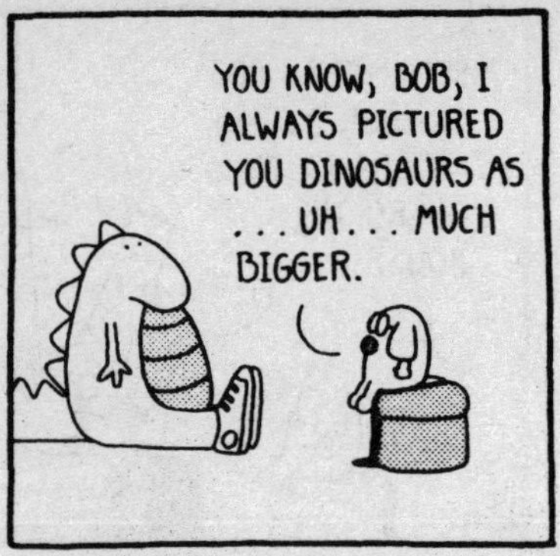
YOU KNOW, BOB, I ALWAYS PICTURED YOU DINOSAURS AS . . . UH . . . MUCH BIGGER.

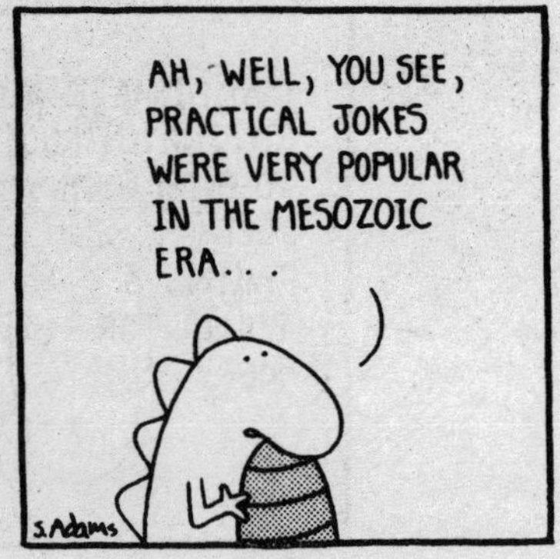
AH, WELL, YOU SEE, PRACTICAL JOKES WERE VERY POPULAR IN THE MESOZOIC ERA. . .
S. Adams

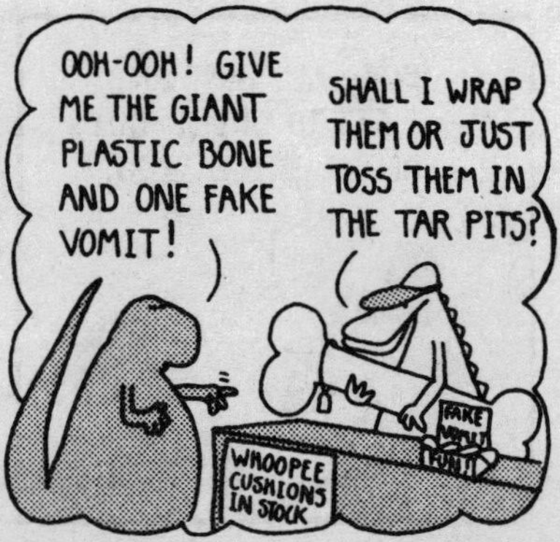
OOH-OOH! GIVE ME THE GIANT PLASTIC BONE AND ONE FAKE VOMIT!
SHALL I WRAP THEM OR JUST TOSS THEM IN THE TAR PITS?
WHOOPEE CUSHIONS IN STOCK
FUN!

HEY! BIG GUY, HOW ARE YA?
IN
OUT
HOW'S THE FAMILY? YOU LOOK GREAT... NICE WEATHER, HUH?
OUT
I HATE OUTGOING MAIL.
DO YOU FISH?

I'VE NOTICED THAT ALL THE COOL GUYS USE GENTLE KIDDING WITH WOMEN.
WOMEN MUST LIKE IT.
EXCUSE ME, MISS, DOES YOUR FACE HURT? IT'S KILLING ME!
Giggle Giggle Snort
THE COOL GUYS MUST HATE IT WHEN THIS HAPPENS TO THEM.
S. Adams

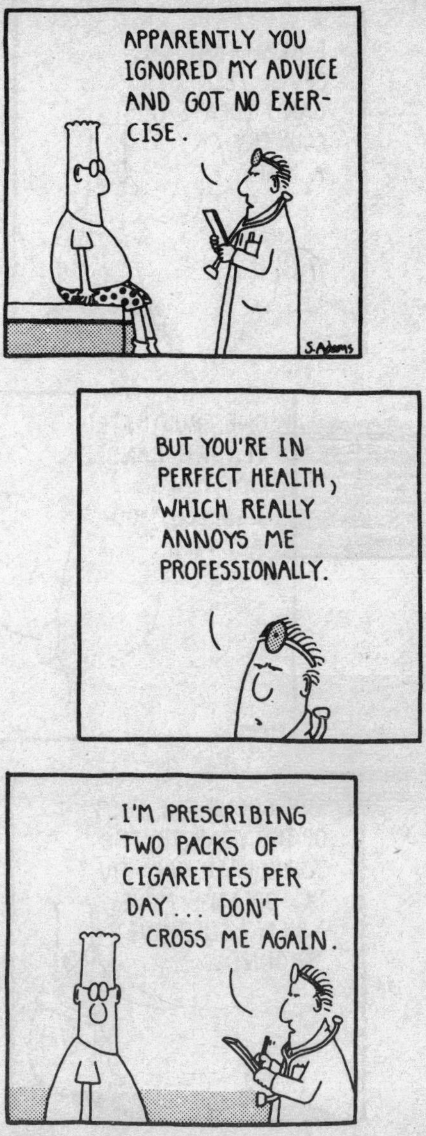
APPARENTLY YOU IGNORED MY ADVICE AND GOT NO EXER-CISE.
S.Adams
BUT YOU'RE IN PERFECT HEALTH, WHICH REALLY ANNOYS ME PROFESSIONALLY.
I'M PRESCRIBING TWO PACKS OF CIGARETTES PER DAY... DON'T CROSS ME AGAIN.

I READ THAT HALF OF ALL TEENAGERS CAN'T LOCATE THIS COUNTRY ON A MAP.
ONE FRUSTRATED TEACHER HANDED OUT MAPS LABELED "YOU ARE HERE."
S.Adams
SHE SPENT THE REST OF THE YEAR TRYING TO EXPLAIN WHY THE "X" DOESN'T MOVE WHEN YOU DRIVE AROUND.

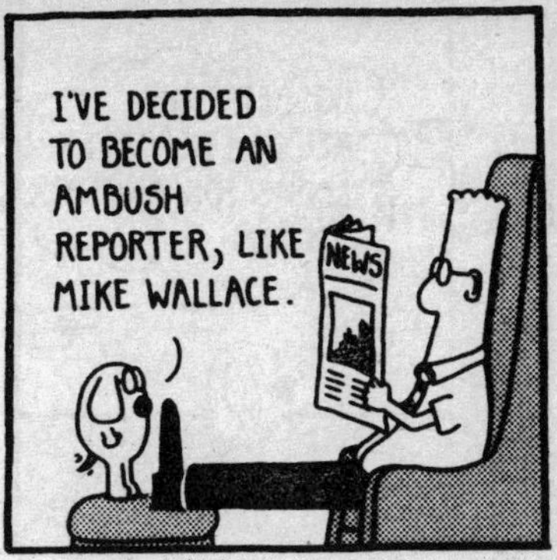
I'VE DECIDED TO BECOME AN AMBUSH REPORTER, LIKE MIKE WALLACE.
NEWS

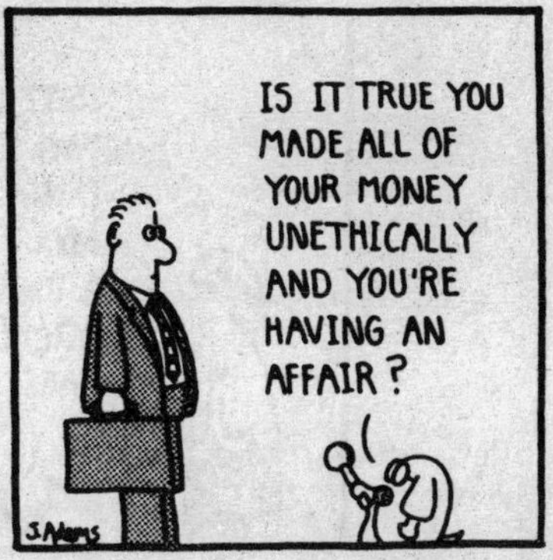
IS IT TRUE YOU MADE ALL OF YOUR MONEY UNETHICALLY AND YOU'RE HAVING AN AFFAIR?
S.Adams

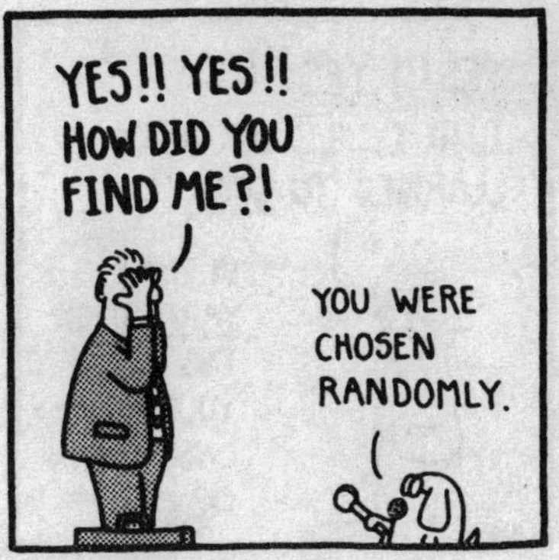
YES!! YES!! HOW DID YOU FIND ME?!
YOU WERE CHOSEN RANDOMLY.

DOGBERT THE AMBUSH REPORTER LOOKS FOR ANOTHER VICTIM.
IS IT TRUE YOU HAVE OFTEN FANTASIZED ABOUT MARRYING A RICH GUY AND DITCHING YOUR CAREER?
YES!!! YES!!!
AND I...I...SECRETLY LEARNED TO COOK!!
IS THAT YARN STICKING OUT OF YOUR BRIEFCASE?!!
S. Adams

JUST A MOMENT, LITTLE GIRL. I'M DOGBERT, THE AMBUSH REPORTER.
IS IT TRUE THAT YOU PRETEND TO BE CUTE IN ORDER TO MANIP-ULATE ADULTS !!
S.Adams
SNIFF
SNIFF
OH, HEY, WAIT... I'M JUST KIDDING. CAN I BUY YOU SOMETHING EXPENSIVE?

EXCUSE ME, YOUNG MAN. MAY I ASK YOU SOME PROBING AND EMBARRASSING QUESTIONS?

IS IT TRUE THAT YOU SPEND A GREAT DEAL OF TIME CONTEMPLATING THE EFFECTS OF FIRE-CRACKERS ON INVESTI-GATIVE REPORTERS?!!

I'LL BET THIS HASN'T HAPPENED TO MIKE WALLACE EVEN ONCE.

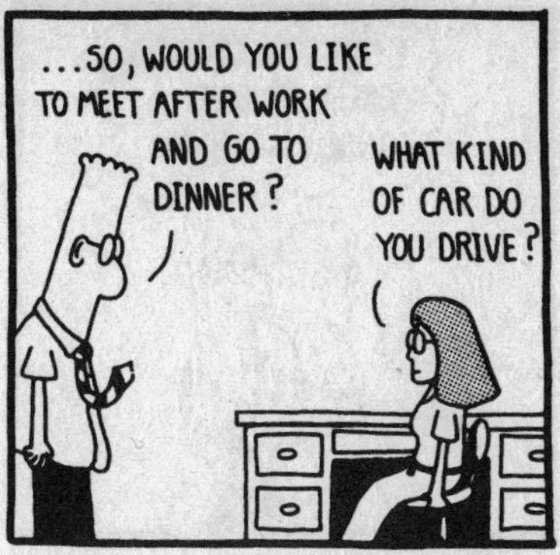
...SO, WOULD YOU LIKE TO MEET AFTER WORK AND GO TO DINNER?
WHAT KIND OF CAR DO YOU DRIVE?

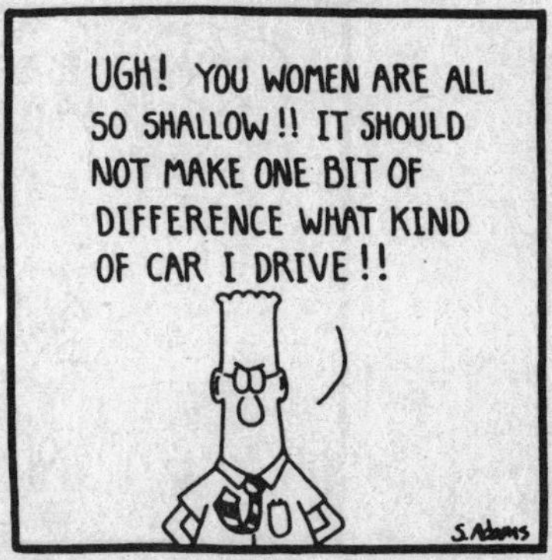
UGH! YOU WOMEN ARE ALL SO SHALLOW!! IT SHOULD NOT MAKE ONE BIT OF DIFFERENCE WHAT KIND OF CAR I DRIVE!!
S. Adams

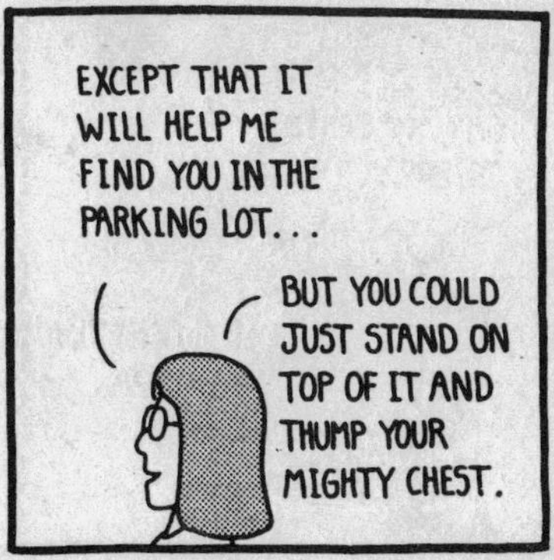
EXCEPT THAT IT WILL HELP ME FIND YOU IN THE PARKING LOT...
BUT YOU COULD JUST STAND ON TOP OF IT AND THUMP YOUR MIGHTY CHEST.

I CAN'T BELIEVE SHE AGREED TO HAVE DINNER WITH ME.
S.Adams
I'M AFRAID TO SAY ANY-THING TO SPOIL THIS MOMENT...
I GUESS I SHOULD SAY SOMETHING TO BREAK THE ICE.
DID I MENTION THAT I'M A WITCH ?

THANKS FOR ASKING ME OUT. MOST GUYS GET SCARED WHEN THEY FIND OUT I'M A PRACTICING WITCH.
THEN THEY SAY SOMETHING I DON'T LIKE AND I END UP TURNING THEM INTO LAWN ORNAMENTS.
S.Adams
THAT'S AWFUL!
TELL ME ABOUT IT... YOU CAN'T BELIEVE HOW TACKY MY LAWN IS NOW.

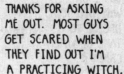

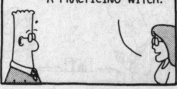

SO...UH... WHY DID YOU DECIDE TO TAKE UP WITCH-CRAFT?
IT COMES IN HANDY.
FOR EXAMPLE, SUPPOSE I WANT TO GET RID OF THIS ANNOYING FLY HERE.
NOW BE A LUV...

YOU'RE BACK EARLY. HOW WAS YOUR DATE?
NOT SO GOOD... SHE'S A WITCH... TURNED ME INTO A FROG.
OOOH! WHEN I THINK ABOUT IT I JUST GET SO...SO...
HOPPING MAD?

DOGBERT, I NEED YOUR HELP. CHECK MY COMPUTER TO SEE IF THERE IS ANY WAY TO REVERSE THE SPELL AND MAKE ME HUMAN!
HMM... "THE ONLY WAY TO REVERSE A "FROG SPELL" IS A KISS FROM A DOG OR A PRINCESS..."
S.Adams
WHAT'D IT SAY?!!
GARGLE. YOU'RE GONNA VISIT LADY DI.

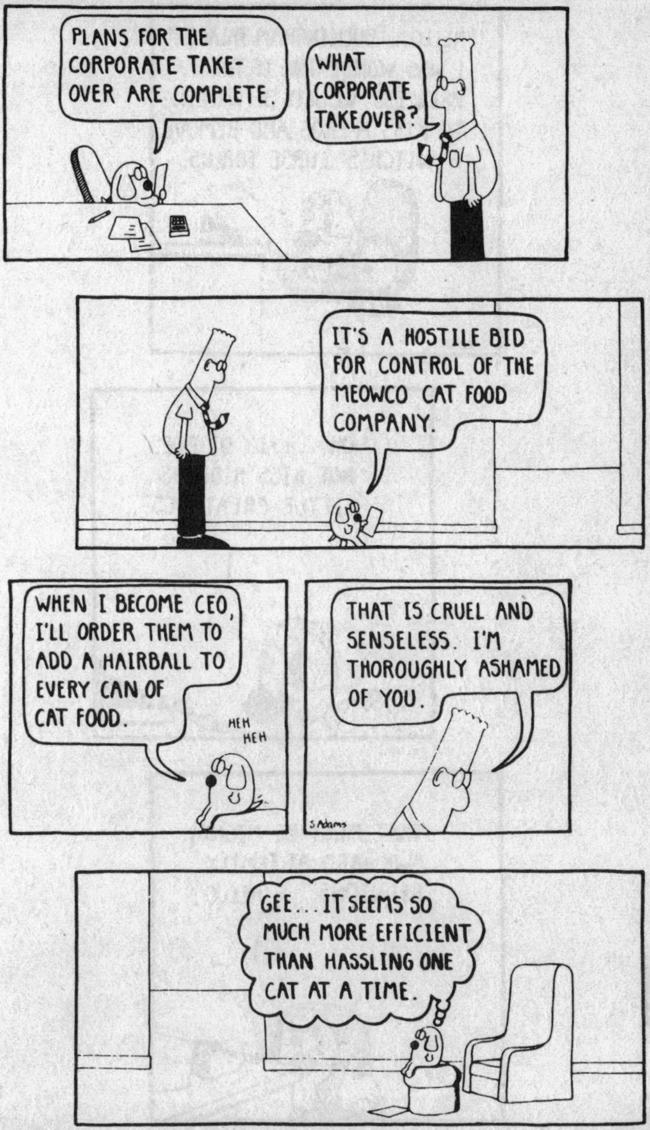
PLANS FOR THE CORPORATE TAKE-OVER ARE COMPLETE.
WHAT CORPORATE TAKEOVER?
IT'S A HOSTILE BID FOR CONTROL OF THE MEOWCO CAT FOOD COMPANY.
WHEN I BECOME CEO, I'LL ORDER THEM TO ADD A HAIRBALL TO EVERY CAN OF CAT FOOD.
HEH HEH
THAT IS CRUEL AND SENSELESS. I'M THOROUGHLY ASHAMED OF YOU.
S Adams
GEE... IT SEEMS SO MUCH MORE EFFICIENT THAN HASSLING ONE CAT AT A TIME.

HELLO... BUCKINGHAM PALACE? I WAS WONDERING IF THE PRINCESS WOULD BE WILLING TO KISS A FROG AND REMOVE A WITCH'S CURSE FOR US.
S.Adams
OH... LADY DI DOES NOT KISS HIDEOUS LITTLE CREATURES...
THAT MUST BE MIGHTY AWKWARD AT FAMILY REUNIONS ... HELLO?

DILBERT NEEDS A KISS FROM A PRINCESS TO REMOVE THE FROG CURSE.
IT'S HOPELESS...
S.Adams
THERE'S ONE CHANCE, BUT WE'LL NEED SOME PROPS.
YOU SERIOUSLY THINK THIS WILL FOOL LADY DI?
I'D WAIT UNTIL SHE'S HAD A FEW MARGARITAS.

NOTE:
SOME NEW READERS OF THIS
STRIP MAY BE CONFUSED BY
THE PRESENCE OF A CHARACTER
WHO LOOKS VERY MUCH LIKE
A POTATO. THE FOLLOWING
COMPARISON SHOULD CLEAR
THINGS UP:

S. Adams

DILBERT (TURNED
INTO A FROG AND
DISGUISED AS
PRINCE CHARLES).

A POTATO

A HANDY RULE FOR TELLING
WHICH ONE IS A POTATO IS
TO LOOK FOR THE PRESENCE
OF GLASSES. ALTHOUGH
POTATOES DO HAVE EYES,
THEY ARE KNOWN TO BE
VAIN AND GENERALLY
PREFER CONTACT LENSES.
KEEP THIS REFERENCE
GUIDE WITH YOU.

BY NOW DILBERT SHOULD HAVE INFIL-TRATED BUCKING-HAM PALACE.
ONE KISS FROM THE PRINCESS AND HIS "FROG CURSE" WILL BE LIFTED...
I JUST HOPE HIS DISGUISE WORKS...
CHARLIE, WHY DOES YOUR BREATH SMELL LIKE FLIES?
UH... I HAD LUNCH WITH A COMMON PERSON TODAY...
S.Adams

I'M JUST A ONE-WOMAN KIND OF GUY.
SOME GUYS LIKE TO PLAY THE FIELD. NOT ME. I'M HAPPY WITH JUST ONE WOMAN.
S. Adams
JUST ONE. UNO. THAT'S BEST FOR ME.
YOU CAN TAKE HER FOR RIDES IN THE SPACE SHUTTLE YOU'LL NEVER HAVE EITHER.

YOUR NEW PROJECT WILL BE VITAL TO THE PERFORMANCE OF THIS COMPANY!
UH-OH
THE MORE HE TALKS IT UP THE STUPIDER THE PROJECT MUST BE.
...HIGH VIS-IBILITY, A CHANCE TO EXCEL AND BE NOTICED!
IN FACT, I STAND TO SALUTE YOU FOR THE JOB YOU WILL BE DOING! YOU'RE WHAT MAKES THIS COUNTRY GREAT!!
DOES THIS HAVE ANY-THING TO DO WITH THE JANITORS' STRIKE?

I'M GOING TO FORM A PERSONALITY CULT TO HONOR ME.
I'LL TAKE EVERYBODY'S MONEY AND MAKE THEM WEAR BATHROBES WITH MY PICTURE ON THE BACK.
S. Adams
WOULDN'T IT BE CHEAPER TO BRAND THEM AND LET THEM RUN NAKED?
AS A RULE, WE'RE NOT TALKING ABOUT ATTRACTIVE PEOPLE HERE.

I'M HOPING YOU WILL ACCEPT ME IN THE DOGBERT CULT.
YOU DO HAVE A STRONG RÉSUMÉ . . .
LOOKS LIKE YOU'VE BEEN FLEECED BY SEVERAL SPIRITUAL LEADERS ALREADY.
S.Adams
I THINK THAT DEMONSTRATES A COMPLETE ABSENCE OF INDEPENDENT THOUGHT.
CAN YOU CHANT ?

WE HEARD YOU'RE FORMING A CULT. CAN WE JOIN?
HMM...
YEAH... I COULD USE SOME ENFORCERS TO HELP ME CONCEAL THE HIDEOUS AND CYNICAL NATURE OF MY ORGANIZATION.
YOU'RE IN...
YES! WE MADE IT!
BOB, SHOULD WE ASK ABOUT THE HIDEOUS PART?

BOB AND DAWN JOIN DOGBERT'S CULT.
YOU TWO ARE IN CHARGE OF SECURITY.
YOUR JOB IS TO NEUTRALIZE ANYBODY WHO QUESTIONS MY MOTIVES.
ACTUALLY, WE HAVE SOME QUESTIONS OF OUR OWN...
OR SHOULD WE JUST NEUTRALIZE OURSELVES?
MAKE IT LOOK LIKE AN ACCIDENT.
S.Adams

UH... DILBERT, COULD WE GET YOUR ADVICE?
WE JUST JOINED DOGBERT'S NEW CULT.
AND HE ORDERED US TO KILL EACH OTHER FOR QUESTIONING HIM.
HMM... MAYBE YOU COULD SHOVE EACH OTHER IN FRONT OF TRUCKS.
S. Adams

HOW DID WE EVER ALLOW OURSELVES TO BE DRAWN INTO DOGBERT'S EVIL CULT?
S. Adams
MAYBE HE HAS STRANGE HYPNOTIC POWERS. MAYBE WE WERE MESMERIZED BY HIS ORATORICAL SKILL.
IT SAYS HERE YOU HAVE BRAINS THE SIZE OF A WALNUT.
WHAT'S YOUR POINT?

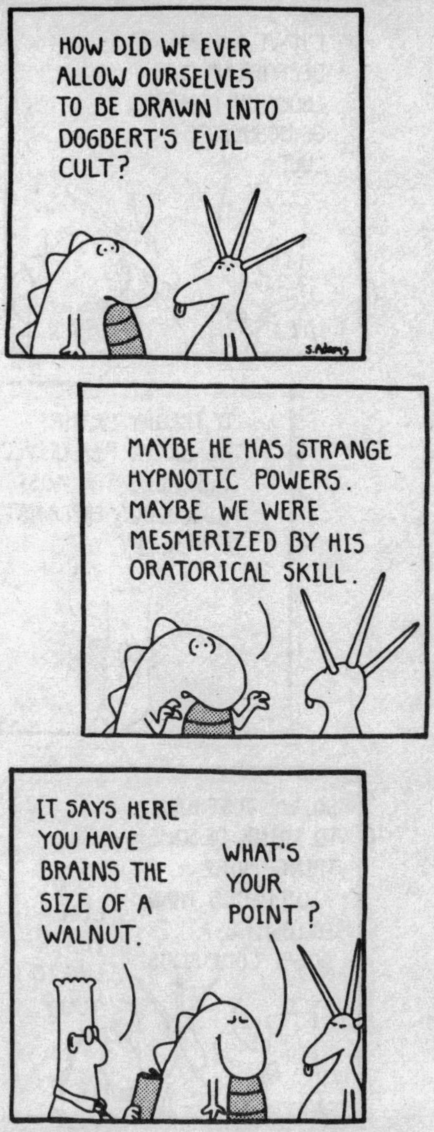

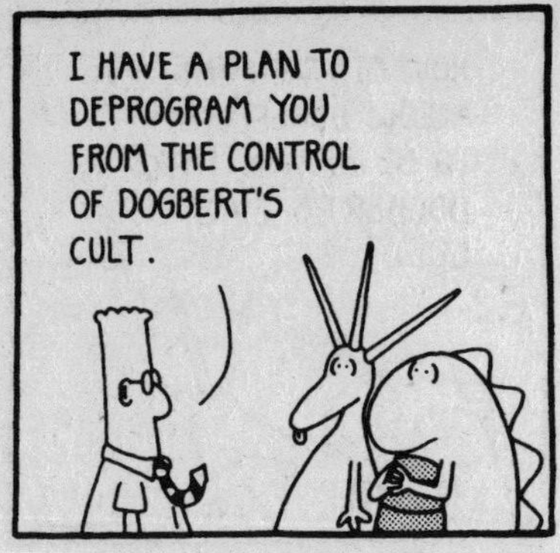
I HAVE A PLAN TO DEPROGRAM YOU FROM THE CONTROL OF DOGBERT'S CULT.

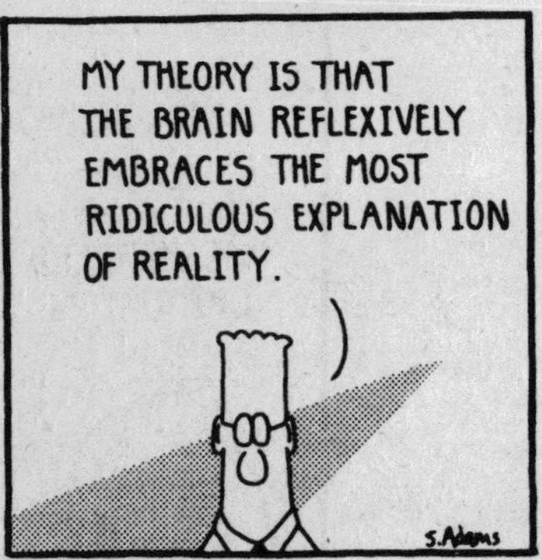
MY THEORY IS THAT THE BRAIN REFLEXIVELY EMBRACES THE MOST RIDICULOUS EXPLANATION OF REALITY.
S. Adams

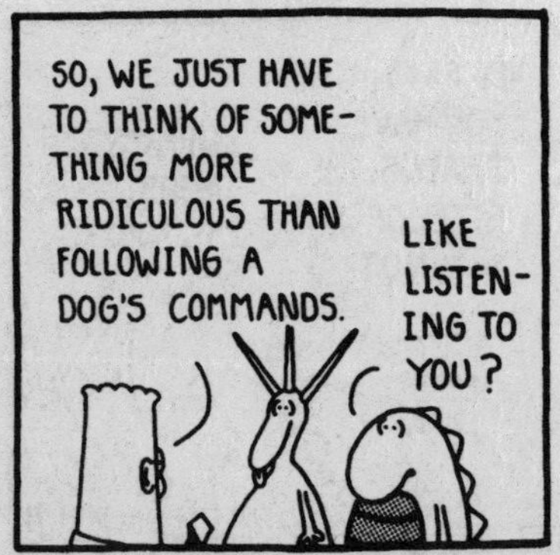
SO, WE JUST HAVE TO THINK OF SOME-THING MORE RIDICULOUS THAN FOLLOWING A DOG'S COMMANDS.
LIKE LISTEN-ING TO YOU?

DOGBERT, WE'VE COME TO RESIGN FROM YOUR CULT.
YOU CAN'T PUSH US AROUND ANYMORE.
RESIGN?!! HA! YOU'RE UNWORTHY! I KICK YOU OUT. THE CULT DOESN'T NEED YOUR TYPE!
S. Adams
NOOO!! TAKE US BACK!!! PLEASE!!!
I THINK THIS EXPLAINS WHY DINOSAURS DON'T RULE THE EARTH.

I THINK YOU'VE TAKEN YOUR CULT IDEA TOO FAR.
WHO SAYS IT'S A CULT?
YOU SAID IT'S A CULT!
THAT WORD HAS A BAD CONNOTATION.
S.Adams
I PREFER TO THINK OF IT AS A BUNCH OF MORONS WHO HAVE NOTHING BETTER TO DO WITH THEIR LIVES.

TODAY ON "GERALDO" OUR ENTIRE SHOW IS ABOUT A DOG WHO STARTED HIS OWN CULT!
ACTUALLY, GERALDO, I DON'T KNOW WHAT YOU'RE TALKING ABOUT.
I LOVE LIVE TELEVISION.

I'M DISSOLVING THE CULT. YOU TWO ARE FREE TO DO AS YOU PLEASE.
WE'RE FREE! WE'RE FREE!
S.Adams
BOY... YOU DON'T KNOW UGLY 'TIL YOU'VE SEEN DINOSAURS DANCE.

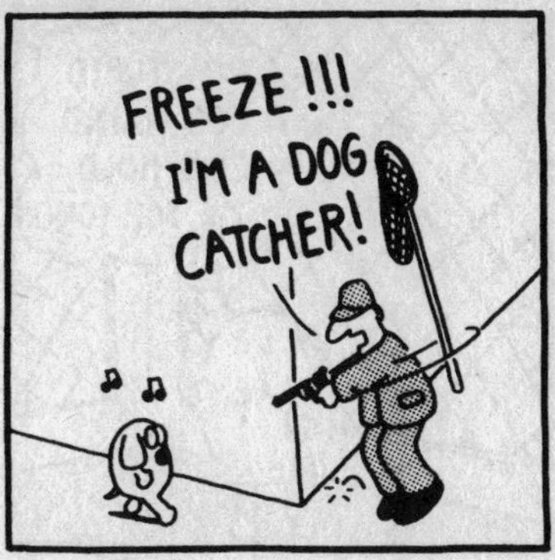
FREEZE !!! I'M A DOG CATCHER!

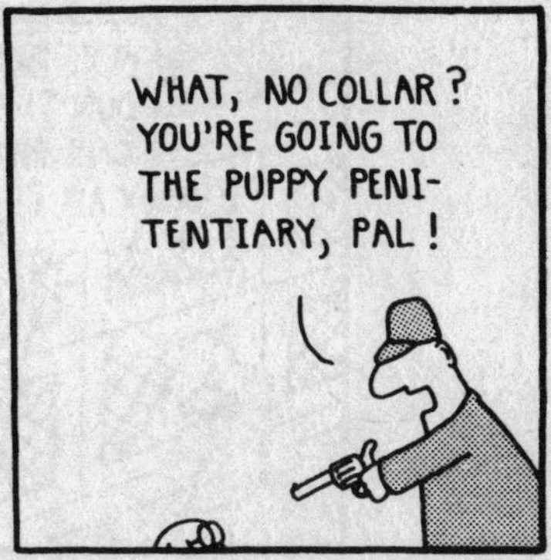
WHAT, NO COLLAR? YOU'RE GOING TO THE PUPPY PENI-TENTIARY, PAL!

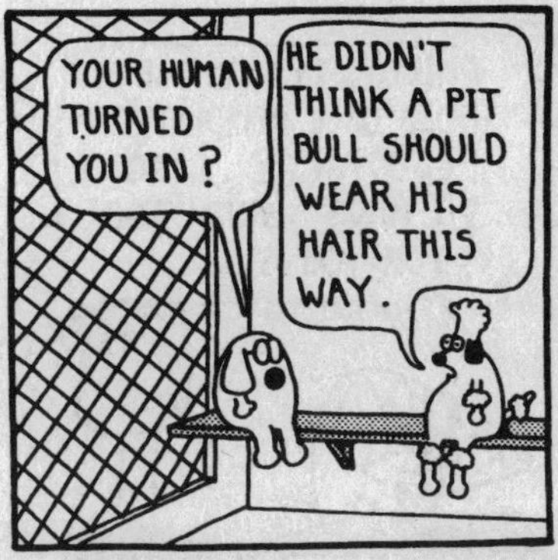
YOUR HUMAN TURNED YOU IN?
HE DIDN'T THINK A PIT BULL SHOULD WEAR HIS HAIR THIS WAY.

NO STUPID DOG POUND CAN HOLD ME FOR LONG.
HEY, SCREW! DON'T I GET ONE PHONE CALL?!
HELLO, IS THIS THE BIG BALL DEMOLITION COMPANY? . . . GOOD, I HAVE A RUSH JOB FOR YOU . . .

DON'T WORRY, KILLER, I'LL GET US OUT OF THIS POUND BY NIGHTFALL.
HOW?
I USED MY ONE PHONE CALL TO CALL A WRECKING COMPANY TO DESTROY THIS PLACE.
THAT SOUNDS DANGER-OUS TO ME.
S. Adams
COMING UP: A NEAR-DEATH EXPERIENCE OR POSSIBLY JUST A STUPID DREAM SEQUENCE.

UH-OH. THAT LOOKS LIKE MY BODY ON THE GROUND.
I MUST BE DEAD. AND THAT LIGHT... IT'S BEAUTI-FUL...
IT MUST BE GOD!!
S. Adams
NEXT: A REALLY BIG LET DOWN.
ZZZ
ZZZ

DOGBERT DREAMS OF DEATH
I'M COMING TOWARD THE LIGHT...
ZZZZ
THE LIGHT... IT'S SO PURE ... SO PERFECT... IT COULD ONLY BE THE LIGHT OF GOD HIMSELF!!
S.Adams
NO. JUST NEW BATTERIES.
GOD HAS A SENSE OF HUMOR? OF COURSE! IT EXPLAINS EVERYTHING.

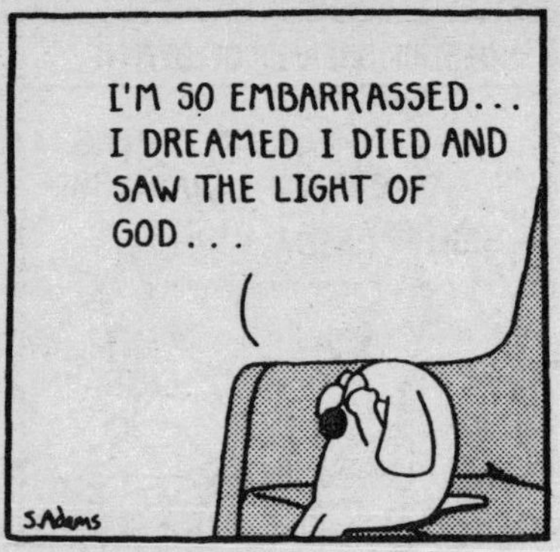
I'M SO EMBARRASSED... I DREAMED I DIED AND SAW THE LIGHT OF GOD...
S. Adams

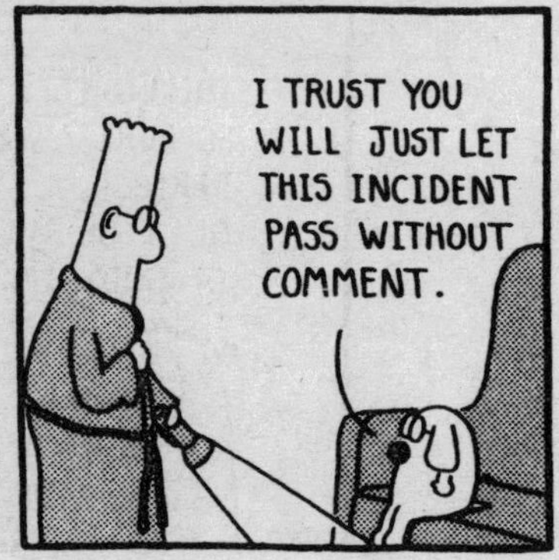
I TRUST YOU WILL JUST LET THIS INCIDENT PASS WITHOUT COMMENT.

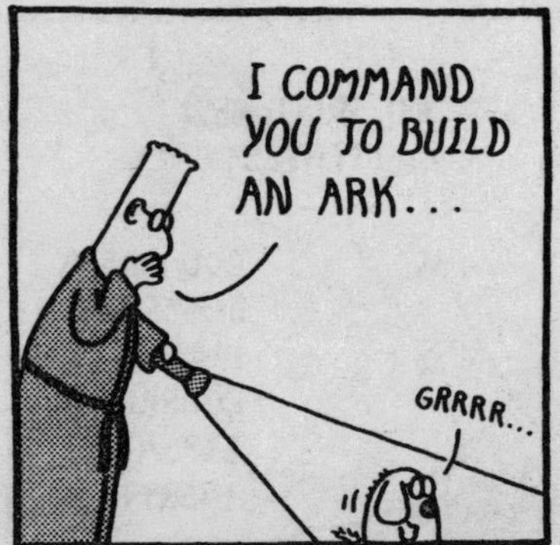
I COMMAND YOU TO BUILD AN ARK...
GRRRR...

THIS COULD BE MY MOST IMPORTANT TECHNICAL ACHIEVEMENT YET. I'LL CALL IT THE "SONIC OBLITERATOR."

HMM... CATCHY.

THIS BABY CAN BLAST A BUFFALO INTO RANDOM PARTICLES IN ABOUT HALF A NANOSECOND.

OF COURSE, IT MIGHT HAVE LIMITED APPLICATION AROUND THE HOUSE.

AT LEAST THE BUFFALOES WILL SHOW US SOME RESPECT.

MAY I PLAY WITH YOUR "SONIC OBLITERATOR" INVENTION?
SURE.
JUST BE CAREFUL. IT HAS A HAIR TRIGGER AND CAN BLOW A TRUCK TO BITS.
NEAT!
YOU HAVE TO SHOW THEM THAT YOU TRUST THEM.
I'LL BE DOWN AT THE POST OFFICE TRUCK YARD.
S. Adams

ON ONE HAND, I KNOW IT'S WRONG TO USE DILBERT'S INVENTION TO BLOW UP THESE EMPTY MAIL TRUCKS.
ON THE OTHER PAW, THIS IS GONNA BE MORE FUN THAN SNEEZING ON STRANGERS.
IT'S A MORAL DILEMMA... BUT I LIKE TO THINK THAT DIFFICULT CHOICES LIKE THIS BUILD CHARACTER.
CLICK

OUR TOP STORY: A DOG WITH GLASSES WAS SEEN BLOWING UP EMPTY MAIL TRUCKS WITH SOME TYPE OF "SONIC OBLITERATOR."
MUCH OF THE CITY IS IN RUINS, AS THE DOG BLASTED THROUGH BUILDINGS TO ESCAPE POLICE AND NATIONAL GUARD PURSUIT.
ON THE PLUS SIDE, WE HAVE A MUCH BETTER SHORTCUT TO THE POST OFFICE.
S. Adams

JUST GREAT... YOU'VE DESTROYED HALF OF THE CITY WITH MY "SONIC OBLITERATOR" INVENTION...
S. Adams
YOU'RE BEING PURSUED BY THE POLICE, FBI AND NATIONAL GUARD...
I TRUSTED YOU. IS THERE ANYTHING YOU'D LIKE TO SAY TO ME?
OH, YEAH, THANK YOU VERY MUCH FOR LETTING ME BORROW THE OBLIT-ERATOR... IT'S BEEN GREAT... CAN I USE IT AGAIN TOMORROW?

LOOKS LIKE THE POLICE FOUND YOUR TRAIL, DOGBERT. YOU'D BETTER HIDE.
S. Adams
WE'RE LOOKING FOR A DOG WHO DESTROYED HALF OF THE CITY. DOES THIS SKETCH LOOK FAMILIAR?
YEAH... IT'S "MISTER POTATO HEAD"... OR MAYBE "ZIGGY."
WE GOTTA GET A BETTER ARTIST.

HERE'S A "HELP WANTED" AD FOR A BABYSITTER.
I COULD DO THAT. KIDS LOVE DINOSAURS.
ONE PROBLEM.
YOUR SPECIES IS KNOWN TO BE CARNIVOROUS.
I'LL PUT "STRICT DISCIPLINARIAN" ON MY RESUME.

HI. I'M BOB. I CALLED EARLIER ABOUT THE BABY-SITTING JOB.
S. Adams
TO BE HONEST, WE DIDN'T KNOW YOU WERE A DINOSAUR WHEN YOU CALLED...
THAT'S OKAY. I DIDN'T KNOW YOU WERE YUPPIE BIGOTS.

...WE SHOULD AT LEAST INTERVIEW HIM. NOBODY ELSE EVEN ANSWERED OUR AD FOR A BABYSITTER.
FRANKLY, BOB, WE'RE CONCERNED THAT YOU MIGHT TRY TO EAT THE CHILDREN.
WELL, OF COURSE, IN THAT CASE THERE WOULD BE NO CHARGE FOR THE EVENING.
HE'S MORE THAN FAIR.

BEFORE WE HIRE YOU AS OUR BABYSITTER, WE WANT TO TEST HOW A DINOSAUR LIKE YOU WOULD RESPOND TO A VARIETY OF EMERGENCY SCENARIOS.
S. Adams
WHAT IF THERE'S A FIRE?
DIAL 911
BURGLARY?
DIAL 911
INJURY?
DIAL 911
POISONING?
DIAL 911
GIANT ASTEROID COLLIDES WITH EARTH AND TRIGGERS AN ICE AGE?
OH, WOW... I'M DRAWING A COMPLETE BLANK HERE...

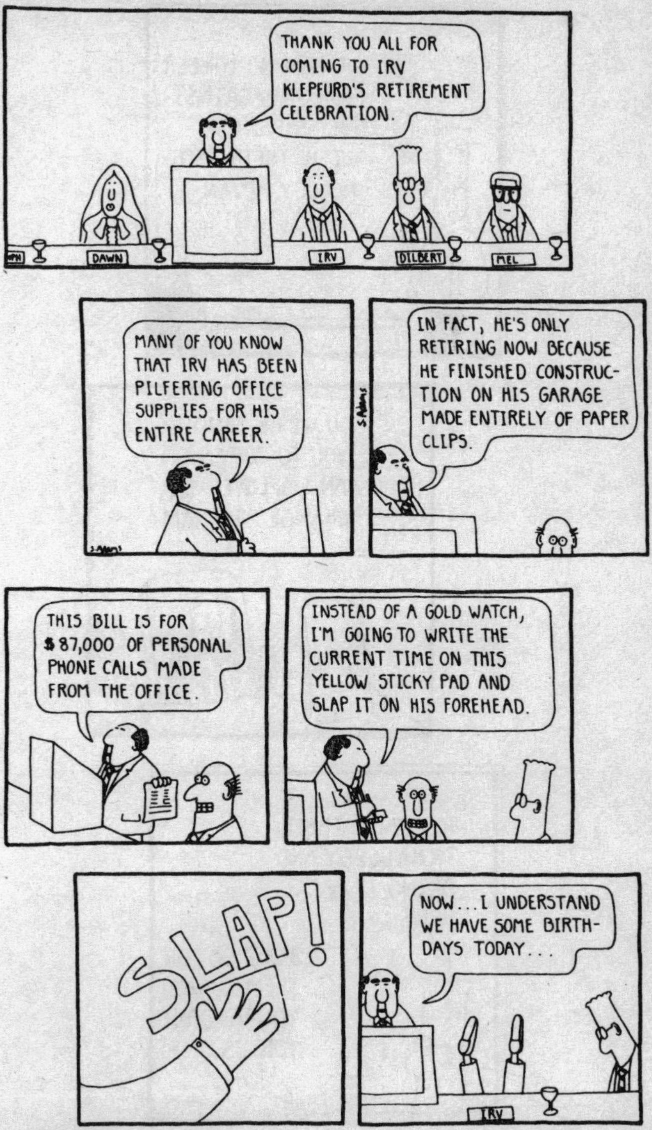
THANK YOU ALL FOR COMING TO IRV KLEPFURD'S RETIREMENT CELEBRATION.
DAWN
IRV
DILBERT
MEL
MANY OF YOU KNOW THAT IRV HAS BEEN PILFERING OFFICE SUPPLIES FOR HIS ENTIRE CAREER.
IN FACT, HE'S ONLY RETIRING NOW BECAUSE HE FINISHED CONSTRUCTION ON HIS GARAGE MADE ENTIRELY OF PAPER CLIPS.
THIS BILL IS FOR $87,000 OF PERSONAL PHONE CALLS MADE FROM THE OFFICE.
INSTEAD OF A GOLD WATCH, I'M GOING TO WRITE THE CURRENT TIME ON THIS YELLOW STICKY PAD AND SLAP IT ON HIS FOREHEAD.
SLAP!
NOW... I UNDERSTAND WE HAVE SOME BIRTHDAYS TODAY...
IRV

WE CAN NO LONGER COMPETE AGAINST THE JAPANESE WITH THEIR TECH-NOLOGY ADVAN-TAGES.
SO WE'RE SENDING YOU TO JAPAN ON AN EMPLOYEE EX-CHANGE PROGRAM.
TO LEARN THEIR TECHNOLOGY AND BRING IT BACK HERE?
JUST DO FOR THEM WHAT YOU'VE DONE FOR US.

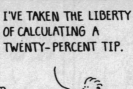

I'VE TAKEN THE LIBERTY OF CALCULATING A TWENTY-PERCENT TIP.

IT'S WRITTEN ON THE BACK NEXT TO A PICTURE OF A SMILING DINER... A FIFTEEN PERCENT TIP IS SHOWN BY THE PICTURE OF A GUILTY-LOOKING DINER.

S.Adams

BELOW THAT IS A PICTURE OF A DINER AND HIS DOG WITH SALAD FORKS IN THEIR BACKS...

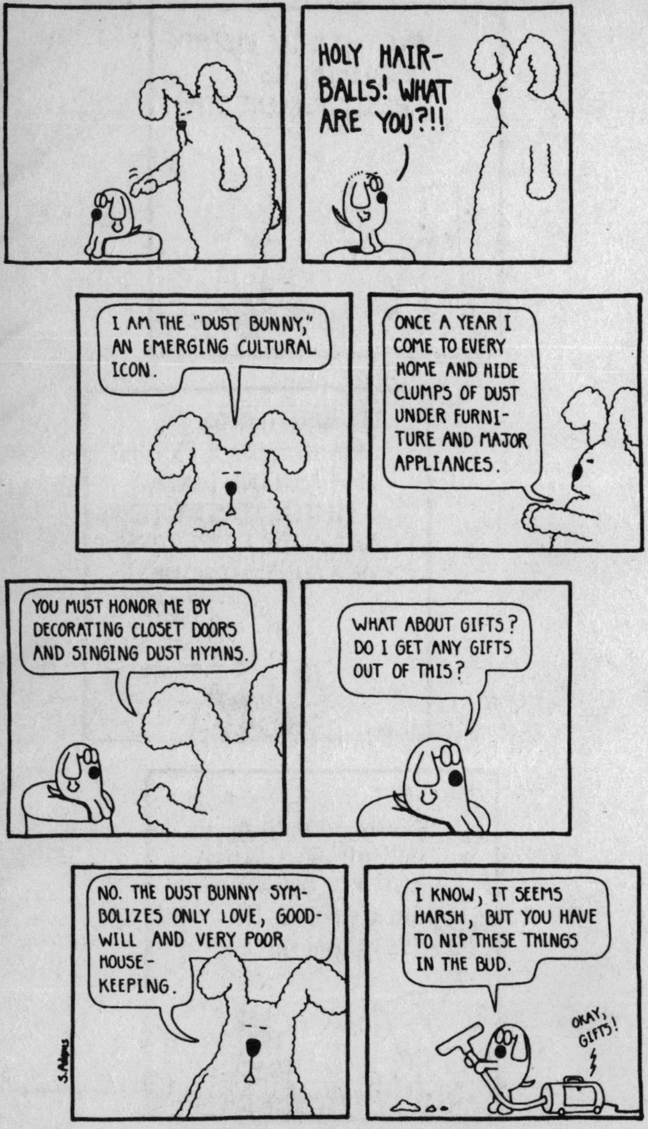
HOLY HAIR-BALLS! WHAT ARE YOU?!!
I AM THE "DUST BUNNY," AN EMERGING CULTURAL ICON.
ONCE A YEAR I COME TO EVERY HOME AND HIDE CLUMPS OF DUST UNDER FURNITURE AND MAJOR APPLIANCES.
YOU MUST HONOR ME BY DECORATING CLOSET DOORS AND SINGING DUST HYMNS.
WHAT ABOUT GIFTS? DO I GET ANY GIFTS OUT OF THIS?
NO. THE DUST BUNNY SYMBOLIZES ONLY LOVE, GOODWILL AND VERY POOR HOUSE-KEEPING.
I KNOW, IT SEEMS HARSH, BUT YOU HAVE TO NIP THESE THINGS IN THE BUD.
OKAY, GIFTS!
S. Adams

HERE WE HAVE A LAB RAT, SPECIALLY BRED TO BE SUSCEPTIBLE TO PEER PRESSURE.
HOW ABOUT A BREWSKI?
I DON'T DRINK.
ALL THE COOL RATS DRINK BEER.
OKAY.
OF COURSE, THERE'S MORE TO SCIENCE THAN JUST HURTING ANIMALS, BUT FRANKLY IT'S THE PART I LIKE BEST.

DOC, WE HAVE TO TALK.
EVERYDAY YOU FEED ME OVER A HUNDRED POUNDS OF MACARONI AND CHEESE . . . AT FIRST I THOUGHT YOU WERE JUST BEING A GOOD HOST.
BUT LATELY I'VE BEEN THINKING IT COULD BE SOME-THING FAR MORE SINISTER.
MACARONI AND CHEESE CAUSES PARANOIA...

I HATE MY LIFE.
IF I EAT ONE MORE TON OF MACARONI AND CHEESE I THINK I'LL DIE...
OF COURSE, THAT MAY BE THE POINT.
TONIGHT I'M GOING "OVER THE WALL."
WAIT... I'M A RAT... I'LL GO THROUGH THE WALL.

WHAT'S THAT NOISE?
SKRITCH
SKRITCH
SKRITCH
IT SOUNDS LIKE A RAT, ESCAPED FROM A NEARBY LABORATORY, CHEWING A HOLE THROUGH OUR FRONT DOOR TO AVOID SURE DEATH FROM A HIDEOUS MACARONI-AND-CHEESE EXPERIMENT.
S. Adams
THAT'S AMAZING.
THESE BABIES AREN'T JUST FOR GOOD LOOKS, YOU KNOW.

GREETINGS, DOG. I'VE COME TO LIVE IN YOUR HOUSE AND ESCAPE FROM MY JOB AT THE LABORATORY.
YOU COULD THINK OF ME AS A POLITICAL EXILE SEEKING SANCTUARY IN A FRIENDLY EMBASSY.
I COULD THINK OF YOU AS A RAT.
OKAY, BUT I DON'T EXPECT ANY SPECIAL TREATMENT.

I WASN'T GETTING ANY RESPECT AT THE LAB . . . I FELT USED.
SURE . . . THE FOOD WAS GOOD - AND LOTS OF IT . . . BUT I DON'T THINK THE PROFESSOR VALUED ME AS AN INDIVIDUAL .
AND A RAT WITHOUT RESPECT IS LIKE . . . LIKE . . .
LIKE YOU.

DILBERT, THIS IS A RAT. RAT, THIS IS DILBERT.
I'VE COME TO LIVE HERE!
HOW LUCKY FOR US. WE WERE JUST SAYING HOW MUCH WE NEEDED A PLAGUE-CARRYING VERMIN TO ROUND OUT THE HOUSEHOLD.
HE DOESN'T HAVE MUCH OF A PERSONALITY...
I USUALLY DROWN HIM OUT WITH THE TELEVISION.

IF YOU'RE GOING TO LIVE HERE, YOU NEED A NAME.
HOW ABOUT "MICKEY"?
NO... BIG TROUBLE. HOW ABOUT "RODNEY THE RODENT"?
HOW ABOUT "BILL THE RAT"?
"VERNON THE VERMIN"?
"RATBERT"
S.Adams

LET ME INTRODUCE YOU TO OUR DINOSAURS, BOB AND DAWN.
COOL!
EEEEK!! A MOUSE!
NOT A MOUSE, A RAT!!
OOPS. SORRY. YOU LOOK KINDA LIKE A MOUSE.
NO OFFENSE TAKEN.

YES ?
I'M LOOKING FOR MY ESCAPED LAB RAT. THE TRAIL LEADS TO THIS HOUSE.
CAN'T YOU JUST USE ANOTHER RAT ?
NO. I'M ON A VERY LIMITED BUDGET.
S.Adams
WHAT WILL YOU DO IF HE DIES ?
CPR

AHAA! THERE'S MY RUNAWAY LAB RAT! I'D RECOGNIZE LITTLE XP-39C^2 ANYWHERE!
ALL IS FORGIVEN. COME BACK TO YOUR JOB AT THE LAB. I LOVE YOU.
S. Adams
HE WAS SPECIALLY BRED TO HAVE NO WILL POWER.
HOLD ME.

GOODBYE, DOGBERT. I MUST RETURN TO THE LAB WITH THE PROFESSOR.
SNIFF
THAT'S STUPID.
HE SAYS HE LOVES ME. THAT MUST BE WHY HE FED ME SO MUCH.
YOU'RE GETTING STUPIDER.
S. Adams
I HAVE TO FOLLOW MY HEART.
HMM... LOVE CAUSES STUPIDITY IN LAB RATS.